OLYMPICS!

by B. G. Hennessy

pictures by Michael Chesworth

PUFFIN BOOKS
Published by the Penguin Group
Penguin Putnam Books for Young Readers, 345 Hudson Street, New York, New York 10014, U.S.A.
Penguin Books Ltd., 27 Wrights Lane, London W8 5TZ, England
Penguin Books Australia Ltd., Ringwood, Victoria, Australia
Penguin Books Canada Ltd., 10 Alcorn Avenue, Toronto, Ontario, Canada M4V 3B2
Penguin Books (N.Z.) Ltd., 182-190 Wairau Road, Auckland 10, New Zealand

Penguin Books Ltd., Registered Offices: Harmondsworth, Middlesex, England

First published in the United States of America by Viking, a division of Penguin Books USA Inc., 1996
Published by Puffin Books, a division of Penguin Putnam Books for Young Readers, 2000

3 5 7 9 10 8 6 4 2

THE LIBRARY OF CONGRESS HAS CATALOGED THE VIKING EDITION AS FOLLOWS:
Hennessy, B. G. (Barbara G.)
Olympics! / by B. G. Hennessy; illustrated by Michael Chesworth.
p. cm.
Summary: Provides a simple overview of the history, preparations, training, and
actual events that are part of the Olympic games.
ISBN 0-670-86522-2
1. Olympics—Juvenile literature. [1. Olympics.]
I. Chesworth, Michael, ill. II. Title
GV721.5.H44 1996 796.48—dc20 95-48127 CIP AC

Puffin Books ISBN 0-14-038487-1

Printed in the United States of America
Set in Texton

Almost three thousand years ago in ancient Greece, athletes tested their skill in sports at games called the Olympics. Every four years men would travel to the arena at Olympia to run, jump, box, wrestle, or race their chariots. Every four years the swiftest women runners ran in the *Heraia*. Enemies would stop battles to allow the contestants to travel safely. During the games, thousands of people watched and cheered for the athletes. The winners were the strongest, the fastest, and the bravest athletes of their time.

Today, all over the world, people are getting ready for the modern Olympics. Everywhere athletes are practicing for the Summer Games.

Runners are running.

Jumpers are jumping.

Throwers are throwing.

Swimmers are swimming laps.

Gymnasts are practicing
somersaults and flips.

Weight lifters are working to
make their muscles strong.

Divers are diving.

Teams are practicing, too.

Soccer, water polo, volleyball, basketball.

Teammates are learning to work together.

Boxers, wrestlers, sharpshooters, tennis players, bicyclists, and horseback riders are all training for the Olympics.

Everyone is getting stronger, faster, and braver.

All over the world, athletes are practicing
for the Winter Olympics, too.

Ice skaters are skating. Skiers are skiing.

Ice hockey teams are learning how to play together.
Bobsled and luge teams are training on their sleds.

There are many other people preparing for the Olympics, too. Workers are busy making flags, basketballs, and hockey pucks. Skis and skates and socks.

Uniforms, sneakers, and goggles.
Helmets, bicycles, kayaks, and
canoes. Tennis rackets and all
kinds of balls. Some workers
are making the Olympic Medals:
gold, silver, and bronze.

Countries take turns hosting the Olympics.
In the Olympic city . . .

Architects are designing huge arenas.
Builders are building ski jumps and pools.
Interpreters are learning different languages
so they can help everyone talk to each other.
Judges and referees are studying the rules.
Farmers are growing flowers to give to the winners.
The Olympic committee is planning each event,
as opening day approaches.

All over the world, planes, trains, buses, and cars are bringing the athletes to the new Olympic village.

For two weeks the village will be
home for thousands of athletes.
Here is where they will eat, sleep,
and make new friends.

Finally, it is opening day.
All the athletes parade into the arena.
A runner carries a torch and lights the Olympic flame.
The Olympic flag is raised.
Blue, yellow, black, green, and red.

Each ring represents a region of the world:
Europe, Asia, Australia, the Americas, and Africa.
Each ring is connected to its neighbor to symbolize
the friendship of the Olympic Games.

Now the Olympics begin.

No more practice.

Hundreds of events.

Thousands of athletes.

Millions of fans.

Who will be the strongest?
Who will be the fastest?
Who will be the most graceful?
Each athlete does his or her best.
Each team plays its hardest.

Every four years, during the Summer Games:

Swimmers race against each other. The divers dive off high boards.

Gymnasts perform their routines.

Runners run short races, long races, and relays.

Some run faster than they ever have before.

Some jump higher. Some throw farther.

All the teams play their matches. The equestrians ride their horses.

Wrestling, boxing, shooting, boating, tennis, cycling—

one by one each event is held.

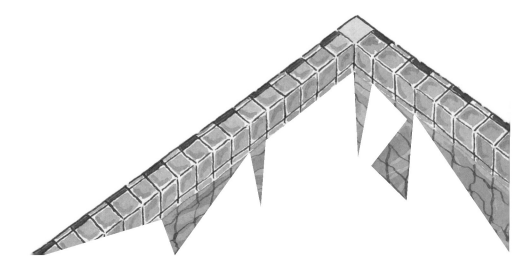

Every four years, during the Winter Games:

Downhill skiers zoom down slopes.

Slalom skiers zigzag fast.

Cross-country skiers ski many kilometers.

Ski jumpers seem to fly off steep snow-covered ramps.

Speed skaters whirl around the ice track.

Figure skaters spin and jump and glide.

A gold medal is given to the winner of each event,
a silver medal to the second-place winner,
and a bronze medal to the third-place winner.
The national anthem of the gold-medal
winner's country is played while the athletes
are given their medals and flowers.

Not everyone can win.
Some athletes lose.
Some cry.
They have worked so long and hard,
and they are very disappointed.
But every athlete, whether he or she
has won a medal or not,
is now an Olympian.

After two weeks, the Olympic Games are over.
The Olympic flag is taken down.
The Olympic flame is put out.
The Olympians say good-bye.
And everyone goes home with new memories,
new friends, and new dreams
from the Olympic Games.